# ATVs
# and Off-roaders

## Lynn Peppas
### Crabtree Publishing Company
www.crabtreebooks.com

# Created by Bobbie Kalman

**Author**
Lynn Peppas

**Publishing plan research
and development**
Sean Charlebois, Reagan Miller
Crabtree Publishing Company

**Editorial director**
Kathy Middleton

**Editor**
Molly Aloian

**Proofreader**
Crystal Sikkens

**Photo research**
Samara Parent

**Design**
Samara Parent

**Production coordinator
and prepress technician**
Samara Parent

**Print coordinator**
Katherine Berti

**Photographs**
Shutterstock.com: back cover, pages 7 (both), 8-9, 10-11, 16, 18, 26, 30; CTR Photos: front cover; PhotoStock10: page 3; Inc: page 4; CTR Photos: page 5; Marcel Jancovic: title page, page 17; Ventura: page 28; Andreas Gradin: page 29; BartlomiejMagierowski: pages 24–25
Thinkstock.com: pages 6, 12, 13, 14, 15, 19, 20, 27
Wikimedia Commons: ©Christian Pichler: page 31; ©U.S. Navy photo by Photographer's Mate 1st Class Arlo Abrahamson: page 21; ©Image by Maas Digital LLC for Cornell University and NASA/JPL: page 22; ©NASA: page 23

**Library and Archives Canada Cataloguing in Publication**

Peppas, Lynn
   ATVs and off-roaders / Lynn Peppas.

(Vehicles on the move)
Includes index.
Issued also in electronic format.
ISBN 978-0-7787-3017-0 (bound).--ISBN 978-0-7787-3022-4 (pbk.)

   1. All terrain vehicles--Juvenile literature. 2. Off-road vehicles--
Juvenile literature. I. Title. II. Series: Vehicles on the move

TL235.6.P46 2012     j629.22'042     C2012-900892-3

**Library of Congress Cataloging-in-Publication Data**

Peppas, Lynn.
  ATVa and off-roaders / Lynn Peppas.
    p. cm. -- (Vehicles on the move)
  Audience: 5-8
  Includes index.
  ISBN 978-0-7787-3017-0 (reinforced lib. bdg. : alk. paper) -- ISBN
978-0-7787-3022-4 (pbk. : alk. paper) -- ISBN 978-1-4271-7941-8
(electronic PDF) -- ISBN 978-1-4271-8056-8 (electronic HTML)
  1. All terrain vehicles--Juvenile literature. 2. Off-road vehicles--
Juvenile literature. I. Title.

TL235.6.P464 2012
629.22'042--dc23

2012004061

# Crabtree Publishing Company

www.crabtreebooks.com    1-800-387-7650

Printed in Canada/042012/KR20120316

**Published in Canada**
**Crabtree Publishing**
616 Welland Ave.
St. Catharines, Ontario
L2M 5V6

**Published in the United States**
**Crabtree Publishing**
PMB 59051
350 Fifth Avenue, 59th Floor
New York, New York 10118

**Published in the United Kingdom**
**Crabtree Publishing**
Maritime House
Basin Road North, Hove
BN41 1WR

**Published in Australia**
**Crabtree Publishing**
3 Charles Street
Coburg North
VIC 3058

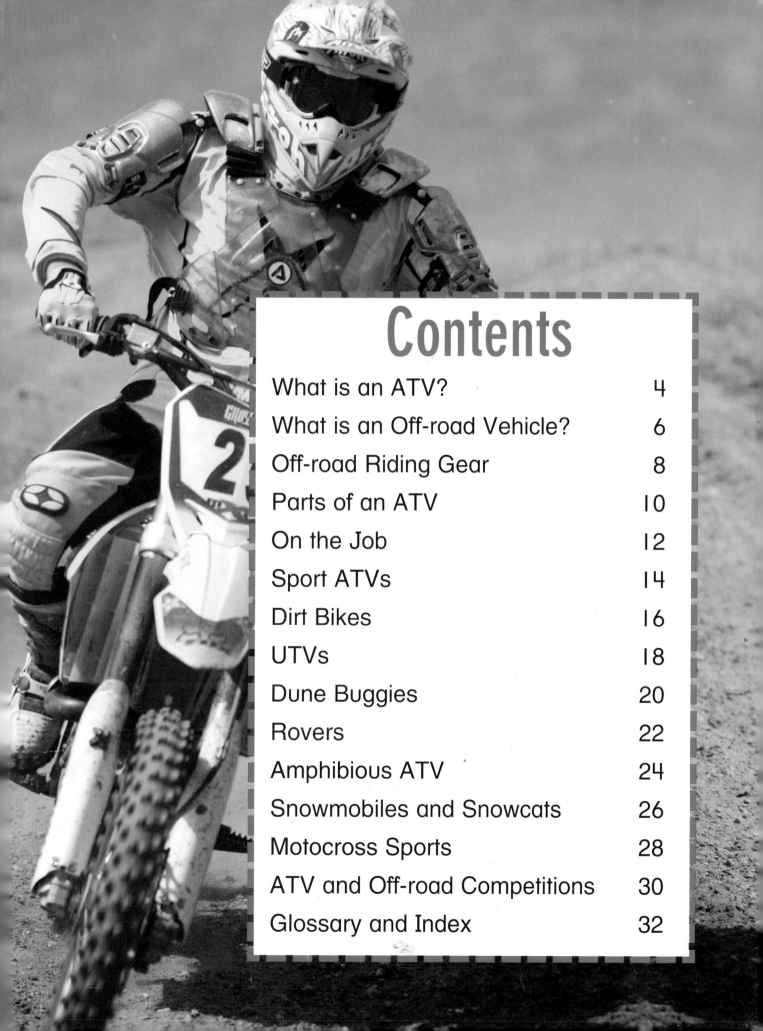

# Contents

# What is an ATV?

An ATV is a vehicle that moves over different kinds of natural **surfaces**. A vehicle is a machine that moves people or things from one place to another. ATV stands for all-terrain vehicle. Terrain means an area of land and its surroundings.

*ATVs carry one rider.*

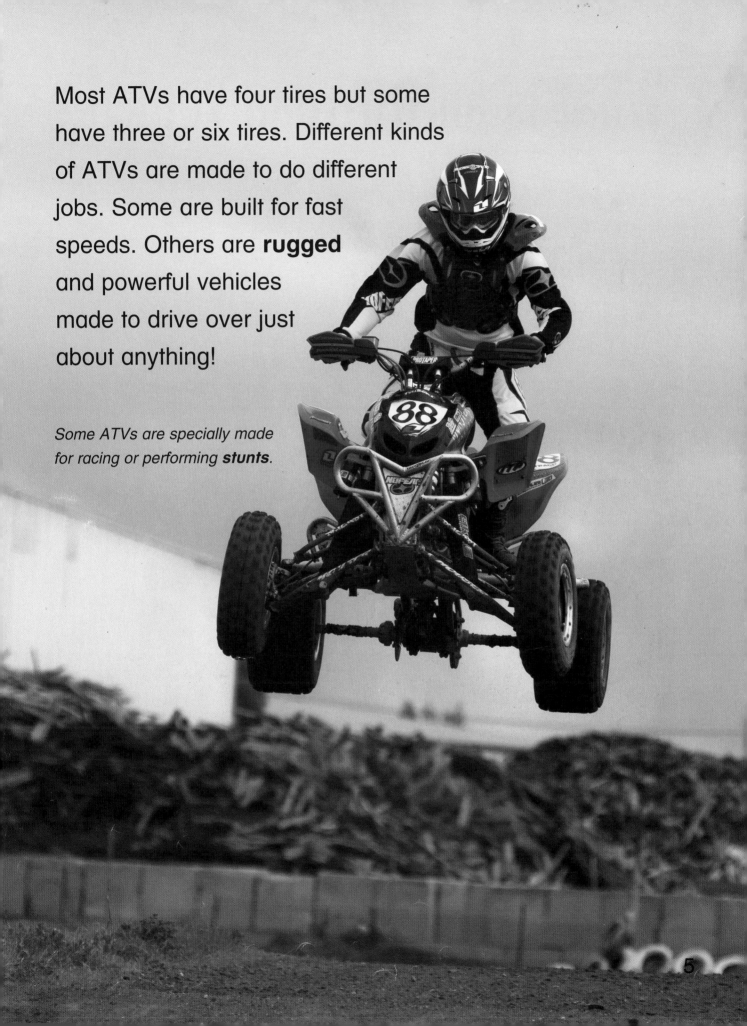

Most ATVs have four tires but some have three or six tires. Different kinds of ATVs are made to do different jobs. Some are built for fast speeds. Others are **rugged** and powerful vehicles made to drive over just about anything!

*Some ATVs are specially made for racing or performing **stunts**.*

# What is an Off-road Vehicle?

Many vehicles such as cars drive on **paved** roads. An off-road vehicle does not need a road. It travels on different kinds of surfaces such as sand, snow, or mud.

*Off-road vehicles can drive over loose gravel and sand or slippery snow and mud.*

Off-road vehicles have large tires with deep **treads**. These tires help off-road vehicles move over surfaces that most vehicles would get stuck in. Some off-road vehicles travel on caterpillar tracks. These are steel plates with ridges.

*Caterpillar tracks are often used on off-road winter service vehicles. Many ski resorts use these vehicles to travel up and down their ski runs.*

# Off-road Riding Gear

Driving over different kinds of surfaces is dangerous. Off-road vehicles can roll over on a rider. For this reason, drivers wear special clothing called gear to protect them from getting hurt.

Riders wear helmets to protect their heads. Special suits cover a rider's full body. The suits keep them warm, dry, or cool in different types of weather. Riders also wear boots and gloves to protect their hands and feet. Knee and elbow pads protect the rider's body in an accident. Goggles or a face shield on a helmet protect the rider's eyes when dirt and mud is flying.

helmet

goggles

gloves

knee pads

boots

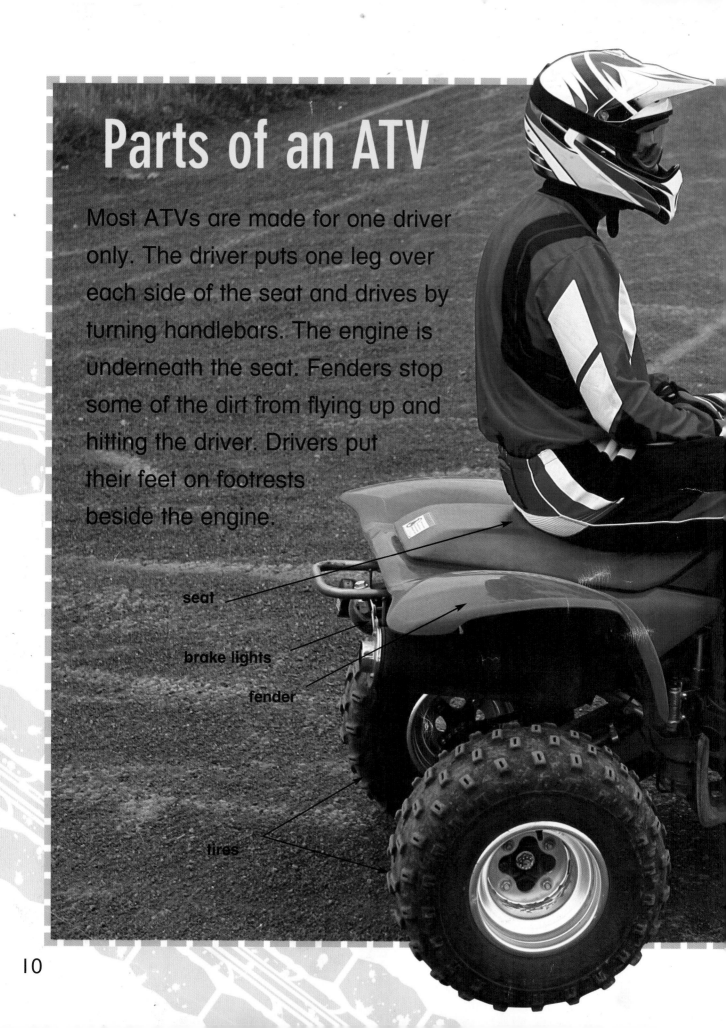

# Parts of an ATV

Most ATVs are made for one driver only. The driver puts one leg over each side of the seat and drives by turning handlebars. The engine is underneath the seat. Fenders stop some of the dirt from flying up and hitting the driver. Drivers put their feet on footrests beside the engine.

seat

brake lights

fender

tires

Large tires with deep tread help ATVs travel over rough surfaces. ATVs have headlights for driving in the dark. Brake lights in the back let other drivers know if the vehicle is slowing down or stopping.

handlebars

headlight

fender

engine

foot rest

# On the Job

Some ATVs are made to work. They help do jobs such as cutting grass, plowing snow, or moving light loads around a farm. They help people get to areas that other vehicles cannot drive to. ATVs that do work are sometimes called **utility** ATVs.

*The tread on the tires of utility ATVs helps to prevent them from getting stuck when plowing snow.*

Utility ATVs are also made for having fun. They can be driven in natural areas such as fields, swamps, or forests. Some have four-wheel drive. This means that each wheel gets power from the engine. If one wheel gets stuck the other three will work to pull it out.

*Going over rocks and sticks in a forest is no problem for a utility ATV.*

# Sport ATVs

Sport ATVs are made to go fast. They give short, fast bursts of speed. They are smaller and lighter than utility ATVs. This makes it easier to do jumps and stunts. They travel speeds of up to 70 mph (110 km/h).

*Sport ATVs travel easily on well-worn trails, dirt tracks, and sand surfaces.*

Sports ATVs are not as rugged as utility ATVs. Many do not have four-wheel drive. They do have better handling. Handling is the ability to steer and make sharp turns.

*Sports ATVs have smaller tires with light treads.*

# Dirt Bikes

A dirt bike is an off-road, two-wheeled vehicle. It gets power from an engine underneath the seat. It is a kind of motorcycle that is made to ride on dirt trails, or paths. Dirt bikes are lighter than motorcycles made for driving on roads. They are rugged vehicles that are made for driving in difficult, natural areas.

*Dirt bikes are used in motocross racing.*

Dirt bikes are sometimes called motocross bikes. Motocross is a word that is made up of parts of two other words. Moto comes from motorcycle and cross comes from cross-country. Cross-country is a kind of race that goes for many miles.

*Motocross races are held in all weather conditions, so motocross bikes have to be able to drive on any kind of surface.*

# UTVs

A UTV is an off-road vehicle made to carry more than just one person. Most UTVs are made to carry two people but others can carry four. UTV stands for utility terrain vehicle. Utility means it is useful and can do work. They are sometimes called a side-by-side.

*Larger ATVs that can carry more than one person are called UTVs.*

A UTV looks like a small car without windows or a roof. Instead of a roof, it has a metal frame called a roll cage. The roll cage protects the people inside if the vehicle rolls over on its sides or roof. A UTV also has handholds so riders can hold on when the driving gets rough.

*Some UTVs have a rear cargo hold or bed. They can carry heavy loads and more than one person.*

# Dune Buggies

A dune buggy is an off-road vehicle that looks like a car with large, wide tires. It carries two or more people. It drives on beaches and sand dunes. A sand dune is a hill made of sand.

*Dune buggies are made for having fun in the sand.*

Soldiers in the U.S. military drive dune buggies called Desert Patrol vehicles (DPV). They are used for search and rescue missions. DPVs carry weapons such as machine guns.

*DPVs are lightweight and can travel quickly. They do not have **armor** to protect them from enemy gunfire.*

# Rovers

A rover is a vehicle made to travel on different planets such as Mars. *Opportunity* and *Spirit* are **robot** rovers that landed on Mars in 2004. They have six aluminum wheels with sharp, metal teeth. They get power from the Sun. They travel over Mars to take pictures with special cameras.

*A Mars Exploration Rover lets scientists study the surface of Mars.*

U.S. Apollo Lunar
rovers were driven
by **astronauts** on
Earth's Moon. They
carry two people.
The tires were made
of different metals
instead of rubber.

*The U.S. Apollo Lunar Rover is
sometimes called a moon buggy.*

# Amphibious ATV

Amphibious means something that can go on land, water, or snow. An amphibious ATV is an all-terrain vehicle that can move on land or in water. Most have six to eight wheels. Others ride on tracks instead of wheels. Most carry two to four people.

In the water, the spinning wheels push the vehicle forward. Amphibious ATVs are controlled with a steering wheel or a control stick.

*Amphibious ATVs go about 2 mph (3 km/h) in the water and about 20 mph (32 km/h) on land.*

# Snowmobiles and Snowcats

Snowmobiles and snowcats are made to travel on snow and ice. Snowmobiles are fast. They carry one or two people. They run on two skis in front pushed by a caterpillar track in the back. Some snowmobiles can go up to 150 mph (240 km/h).

*Snowmobiles are used for work, sports racing, or just having fun in the snow.*

A snowcat is larger than a snowmobile. It carries two or more people in an **enclosed** area. Most run on two large tracks, but some run on four smaller tracks. Snowcats are often used at ski resorts to move and smooth out the snow on ski and snowmobile trails.

*Snowcats are often called "trail groomers" because they **groom** the trails at ski resorts.*

# Motocross Sports

Motocross is an off-road vehicle race. It is held on a dirt racetrack. Motocross events are held outdoors in all kinds of weather conditions. Motocross riders race through natural **obstacles** such as steep hills. They race to get to the finish line first.

*Motocross racing is a popular sport in North America and Europe.*

Both off-road motorcycles and ATVs **compete** in sports such as motocross. Supercross is a sport in which motorcycles race on human-made dirt tracks inside stadiums. During motocross freestyle competitions, riders get points for performing jumps and stunts instead of racing.

*It takes many years of practice for motocross riders to learn to perform stunts such as special jumps.*

# ATV and Off-road Competitions

Enduro is an off-road vehicle competition held on rugged outdoor paths and trails. Riders must get to an area called a checkpoint at a certain time. If they get there too early or late they lose points. Riders drive through rugged terrain such as streams, hills, and mud.

*ATV Mud Nationals is an ATV race through muddy terrain.*

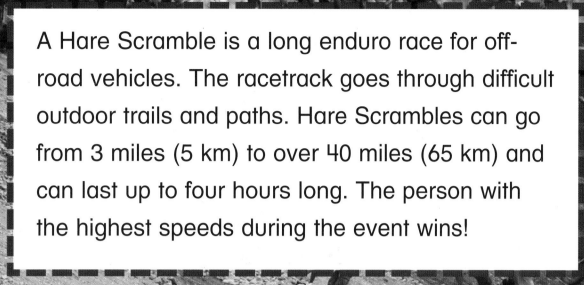

A Hare Scramble is a long enduro race for off-road vehicles. The racetrack goes through difficult outdoor trails and paths. Hare Scrambles can go from 3 miles (5 km) to over 40 miles (65 km) and can last up to four hours long. The person with the highest speeds during the event wins!

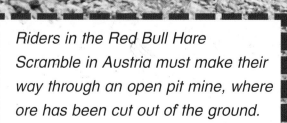

*Riders in the Red Bull Hare Scramble in Austria must make their way through an open pit mine, where ore has been cut out of the ground.*

# Glossary

**armor** A protective covering

**astronaut** A person who travels in space

**compete** A test against others in a certain skill or race

**enclosed** To close in with solid walls made of glass or other materials

**groom** To make the appearance of something look nicer by cleaning, smoothing, or combing it

**obstacle** Something that stands in the way

**pave** To make a path or roadway by laying down asphalt, stones, or concrete

**robot** A machine that can do the job of a human

**rugged** Built to be strong and able to withstand rough conditions

**stunt** A trick or performance that takes great skill to do

**surface** The outside or top layer

**tread** Tall ridges or bumps on a tire helping it move in all kinds of terrain

**utility** Being useful and able to do work

# Index